I0191373

At the Hut of the Small Mind

Other Recent Books by Sanford Goldstein

Tanka Left Behind:
Tanka from the Notebooks of Sanford Goldstein
Keibooks 2014

This Short Life: Minimalist Tanka
Keibooks 2014

Tanka Left Behind 1968:
Tanka from the Notebooks of Sanford Goldstein
Keibooks 2015

Four Decades on My Tanka Road
Winfred Press 2012

This Tanka Whirl
Winfred Press with Clinging Vine Press
2001 – 2015

At the Hut of the Small Mind:

A Tanka Sequence

✧

Sanford Goldstein

———

A WINFRED PRESS BOOK

At the Hut of the Small Mind
a tanka sequence
Second Edition

Winfred Press
364 Wilson Hill Road
Colrain, MA 01340
http://larrykimmel.tripod.com

"a sketch of trees," drawing by Kazuaki Wakui.
Copyright © 2015 by Kazuaki Wakui. Used by permission.

Cover art by Kazuaki Wakui
Cover design by Larry Kimmel

All rights reserved
under international
&
Pan-American conventions.
Published & printed in the USA.

ISBN-13: 978-0-9864328-1-1

Copyright © 2001 – 2015 by Sanford Goldstein
All rights reserved.

Dedicated to

Joy McCall

&

M. Kei

At the Hut of the Small Mind
A Tanka Sequence

1992

Publisher's Note

Though "At the Hut of the Small Mind," is contained in Sanford Goldstein's collection, "Four Decades on My Tanka Road," there has been a continued interest in reprints of the individual books included in that collection. Winfred Press was honored to make available one of these classics of the English-language tanka tradition, "This Tanka Whirl," and now we are twice blessed in being able to publish this new edition of, "At the Hut of the Small Mind," with marvelous new cover art, *"a sketch of trees,"* by Kazuaki Wakui.

Larry Kimmel
Winfred Press
2015

Introduction to
At the Hut of the Small Mind

In July 1982, I traveled to Matsuyama on Shikoku Island to visit the nearby farm of Masanobu Fukuoka, the famous Japanese farmer whose book on natural farming, *The One-Straw Revolution*, I carried with me. An editor of a small American press had asked me to interview Mr. Fukuoka. I knew a little about Mr. Fukuoka's Zen experience, and since I had been interested in Zen Buddhism for at least twenty years and since a Zen master had lived in my house in Indiana on two separate occasions of a year each, I went to Shikoku with trepidation—I would be courting difficulties and the inevitable contradictions that surface in any Zen-oriented world.

Since my spoken Japanese succeeds only on the most mundane levels, I planned my list of some twenty-eight or so questions, planned them with the help of two Japanese friends in Niigata, where I had been living and teaching the past two years. That list I no longer have, for Mr. Fukuoka confiscated it without my ever getting beyond the first question, which he claimed had to be answered before any of the others could be. That question concerned itself with *satori*, or enlightenment, and since my own little breakdown of the written Japanese character for *satori* included five mouths in order to explain the emotion behind *satori*, I was aware of the difficulties I would be encountering by posing that question first. A young Japanese who was at the farm to learn Mr. Fukuoka's methods of Japanese farming and perhaps to translate Mr. Fukuoka's latest book into English (I was never quite certain) sat by me to pass on in English the various statements made by Mr. Fukuoka.

Those three nights and four days I spent at Matsuyama remain memorable—days that were among the most difficult I had spent on my five two-year trips to Japan during the last thirty-two years. It was a period in which I felt I was throwing off much of the clutter (and ease) of the modern world. I was of course frightened and frustrated, and yet I realized I was in the middle of something crucial to life, my own and that of other persons, something ambiguous and beckoning and building. My bare cabin without electricity or running water with an easy accessibility to all that crawls or flies in the outside world, my keyless door and battered screens, my pile of damp *futon*—all that found me groping in darkness after a long first-night session with the farmer and some family members and neighbors and disciples. I was obviously the *gaijin*-foreigner who had come to ask questions, not someone there to work at natural farming.

Later I helped with meals, with cleaning the kitchen floor and low table we ate at, with sweeping and peeling. It was not the KP of my remote life back in the forties. Throughout I felt something of *mu* (interpreted audaciously as I write this introduction as Buddhism's complex yet rich nothingness), of *sabi* (acceptable human loneliness), of *wabi* (the preciousness of old things in all their bare limitations). I remember feeling that even Matsuyama's hills were *wabi*, an obvious poetic-license-*ism*. There were natural peaches, natural rice fields, natural tangerines, and natural summer-*mikan* (unlike anything tangerine in the world with their *shibui* rough-textured shapes and skins), and of course the world was *shiori*, effectively and variously ambiguous on several different levels.

I had come to interview, but only occasionally did I meet Mr. Fukuoka, who appeared and disappeared with strange regularity. I thought he had given me more attention than I deserved in that long three-hour nighttime session in which I had felt like something out of Breughel watched by more than twenty-four eyes. My interviewless-interview found me less a questioner than an examiner of this American self sometimes defecating in a shed under rains that seemed to proclaim some antediluvian connection. But if I saw less of my famous Zen farmer, I saw more of Rebecca, an American from the East Coast studying natural farming, yet more concerned, I felt, with trying to find the Zen way, the Gateless Gate, the magic formula that somehow allows one to walk this tightrope life without falling down. There was also that young Japanese translator (Jiro I shall call him) who every now and then sat poring over Japanese texts. It was odd the third day out to be invited by a group of four young workers, including Rebecca and Jiro, to spend a long rain-filled afternoon and long long evening together, the first at a famous Japanese hot spring bath on the island and then, as if to reinforce the irrationalities of my journey, at a disco bar.

I was actually torn between staying longer at the farm or spending a full week in Kyoto as I had originally planned. But another American visitor suddenly arrived to help me decide to leave. Late in the morning of my fourth day I walked the long muddy road down to a spot where taxis maneuvered along the highway to the airport.

I had no advance plan to write *At the Hut of the Small Mind*, but I had, ever since 1964, kept up what I call my tanka diary. Since I have almost never counted out the traditional thirty-one syllables in writing my tanka poems, it has been easy to continue framing tanka over the years, yet it has always been hard to come up with a good one. At any rate, I knew in advance that I'd be adding poems to my tanka diary, but I hadn't expected to be so on my own in the hut I lived in. I had never before so vividly experienced the limits of my own quite limited self.

And so this tanka sequence: *At the Hut of the Small Mind*. For quite a long long time, more than a decade in fact, I had thought I was writing tanka sequences, but actually I was writing clusters of poems around a single event or experience or person or thought or feeling. It is not my intention to discount those earlier efforts. But for the last five years I had been studying and translating Mokichi Saitō's *Shakkō* (*Red Lights*) with my longtime tanka-translator-collaborator, Professor Seishi Shinoda, and it was through our joint study that I came to realize the dramatic impact of a tanka sequence with its beginning, middle, and end toward some new awareness of the self and/or the world. Mokichi's dramatic night-run entitled "Sad Tidings," the run made just after he learned of the death of his famous teacher Sachio Itō, is perhaps the most famous tanka sequence in Japanese—unless it is Mokichi's sequence on the death of his mother. Whether or not my own tanka sequence is perhaps the first tanka sequence in English by a foreigner is of little consequence, but that it is at least a true tanka sequence pleases me, consisting as it does of the day before my trip to Shikoku, the trip to Matsuyama, the four-day stay at the farm, and the following twenty-four hours in Kyoto.

Perhaps a note of clarification is in order: Mr. Fukuoka calls his method of farming do-nothing farming. While this is misleading since a great deal of labor does go into his methods, I believe he means by it his protest against the excessive procedures modern farmers are forced into complying with for their yields. A devoted advocate of natural farming, Mr. Fukuoka has gained the admiration of a large following.

Sanford Goldstein
West Lafayette, Indiana
December 1985

At the Hut of the Small Mind

devouring
these supermarket cakes
as if tomorrow's
trip
may be my last!

wanting
tonight's
window gaze
an almost-*satori*—
and still only this neon, only this car glare

I pass rice fields,
tiled roofs,
pine, and all the rest;
oh, Japan,
my passing is a passing through

a taxi maze
among
these Matsuyama hills—
until at last
the farm! the farm!

in his rubber raincoat
stark
against white hair
and drooping specs,
the solidity of master?

on the way up
to the mountain hut
the Zen farmer
crushes
a tangerine pest

they give me
food—
I eat
napkinless,
chopsticks without Japanese points

through
this candle-
glow
the eyes
of my natural farmer

around the table
of this mountain hut
our Zen farmer
talking his way
through *mu*

I toss out
a theory
in this Zen hut,
but how real
the brown rice ball in my hand

I zigzag
my way
through theoretical Zen,
hurling my smile
at the master's face

first night:
in the dark
I stumble for a place
to send my urine
natural

how many before me
have found in this mountain hut
moths clinging to corners,
mosquitoes
over this July flesh?

how bare
this mountain hut,
my unwashed body
reduced
to summer smell

voices distant
from my mountain hut
and the long long
cry
of falling rain

the flesh clings
tighter still
as if to tell me
this world is smell,
is touch

a universe
of crawling, flying,
sounding
ambiguities:
insomnia in my mountain hut

that wing
brushed
by candleflame,
and still it fluttered,
still it flew

I am a lump
of thought
this fragmented night
of insect cry
and crawl

I listen
for the soundless—
oh, you analyst,
can't you hear?
can't you smell?

I too
am Basho,
fleas
and that urine smell
in this mountain hut

up this mountain
I came
with my usual
bag
of dishrag servilities

in a corner
tacked
to the mud wall
of my mountain hut,
Mother Teresa

it was roosters
at morning light-fall—
how joyous
even that crack
diagonal

is it
with rain water
I wash?
first morning
in these Matsuyama hills

outside
my hut
where I piss,
am I stepping on radish,
on burdock?

it's by candlelight
and perpetual
cock-crow
I write
my morning poem

in the morning's
candlelight glimmer,
I sweep
these mountain hut
mats

no god
came down
to tap my shoulder,
to say
there's a primitive world

the master
gathers the young,
and by candlelight
dissects
their various worlds

chickens
with legs
on solid ground:
this morning world
at my Matsuyama hut

is it coffee
withdrawal
giving me
this huge split
at the back of my skull?

in this Hut
of the Small Mind,
I'm made
to read
about "knowing"

why I came:
the Zen farmer
asks twice,
three times,
as if my own koan's in it

where's the talk
at breakfast
poking these chopsticks
into *miso* soup,
vegetables, rice?

the others
my Zen farmer led
to practicalities,
me to abstractions
in the Hut of the Small Mind

sounds
of labor in those fields,
sounds
of insect cry,
and, of course, cock-crow

how vivid
that spider
in its lair
I urinate
by

at least
Mother Teresa
smiles at me
from the mud wall
in my Hut of the Small Mind

for hours
I lay
on my hut *futon*
till
even the candleglow waned

as if the world
out there
not nature enough,
a picture of a bird
nailed to my hut's wall

I walk
to the natural rice fields
and back,
I write
my natural poem

green and more green
and greener
still,
these tangerine leaves
in the July rain

the cool
of rain,
July relief
in my Hut
of the Small Mind

not a single complaint
do I hear
from these blades of grass
bombarded
by afternoon rain

all day
in this hut,
mind poring
over the abstract prose
of this man of Zen

a mountain child
in this Hut
of the Small Mind,
I wrap the dampness
round

that bee
stayed and stayed
as if it too
sought shelter
from the July flood

the hills
are *wabi,*
and there's a *shiori* smell
in this Hut
of the Small Mind

communal chopsticks,
and the tips
they mouth
poked into pickles
noodles, rice

the daylight's
long in its descent;
it's by gray shadow
I write
my pre-candle poem

ugly
as facial scars
this *natural* summer-tangerine,
and how bitter
on my tongue!

it might be
Rembrandt:
candleglow shadow
and a student
over his text

only English
spoken round
the mountain hut table—
oh, how silent
is my Japanese

into peyote, he tells me,
and all the rest,
that huddled Japanese
translating the master's
mu

dear Rebecca,
cursing your own people,
you'll never Zen
the long, the lonely
road

from communal vegetables
and rice,
how solitary
the wet night walk
back to my mountain hut

gaining
at least
a two-day growth
of beard
in my Hut of the Small Mind

clutching
bank kleenex
as I squat:
I hear rain slanting
against the shed

I came,
it seems,
to write solitary poems
in my Hut
of the Small Mind

these burly
summer-*mikan*
might be sumo wrestlers
waiting
at ringside

do these pine-tree cutters
on their trees
before the noodle shop
sometimes look at these Matsuyama hills,
these fields of rice?

Sōseki,
you came to these
Matsuyama hills,
chucking away
careers

it's *wabi*
of course:
the old tangerine
crate
against the hut's mud wall

modern civilization?
a black butterfly
in from the rain
through my mountain hut's
battered door

eating
the peach,
I wonder
how natural
it is

this natural
peach
with its natural color
and natural worm,
can I suck it natural?

eating my peach
in the quiet rain,
I listen
to the master's
verse

how minute
the complexities
of even this small world
round
the morning meal

with a rag
I wipe the kitchen floor
wood;
and with a rag
I wipe it again

one sharp verbal blow
from the master
straight at the bull's-eye
of her desire:
Rebecca's tears

this rice bowl
I hold
in the rain—
oh, I want to rinse
after the floss!

back
propped against a wall:
I prepare
to listen
to light

same meal,
same faces,
same chopstick plunge,
and still, still,
this mountain hut life

no waiting
for guests
or for love
at my Hut
of the Small Mind

a motley crew,
some bearded, some in battered
work-a-day clothes,
we make our own way
from these mountain huts

at last
at the public bath
a public back wash
and my hot spring
soak!

how multiple
the uses of my mountain
towel,
sometimes for washing,
sometimes for rain

lolling
in their genital
towels,
these hot spring
discussants

it was
a day
of stories by the young
of their troubled
trips

on the disco
floor
in the armless arms
of the young,
I remember other backs, other faces

they are young
and young and young,
their mountain farm energy
even in their dappled
disco dance

how they peered
at the disco bill
until "grandpa"
pulled out
a ten thousand

told
I'll be a good gramp:
it's not
with much delight
I look at Rebecca's young face

nothing
to catch, to clutch,
though I extend
my hand
this disco night

it's in pouring
rain
I stick out my thumb
to bum
a midnight ride to my hut

again
clutching bank kleenex,
I squat—
was it ages ago
I foretold Buddha's shitstick?

at Natural Farm
is it all futile,
this attempt
to let it all
hang out?

my body
unmasks
in candleglow
the rain
down down

trying to make up
my *Namu Amida Butsu's*
on these missed mountain nights,
I give the dead one
several extras

interfering rain,
how will I make
that slippery way
down the mud
with my tomorrow bag?

a drenched chicken
pecking
at splashes
before the mountain hut
kitchen

woodgathering
in rain,
Rebecca in her blue poncho:
I have scribbled
my morning poem

my chopsticks
dig
into the communal salad:
final breakfast
at Do Nothing Farm

I taste
this potato
in gruel;
I savor the salt
in this pickled plum

at the master's
feet,
two Americans,
one Japanese,
and a white hen

like
a Don Quixote
with a Chinese beard,
the master came,
the master went away

like masters
of Zen,
appearing, disappearing:
three chickens
at Do Nothing Farm

that mud
on your nose,
Rebecca,
tells me
this world is right

at the hot spring, Jiro,
you did not cover
your physical self,
but what you left covered, Jiro,
was immense

urinating
from my hut door,
I too join
this rain
on green leaf

in this natural world
tears, sighs, blows,
all faded,
faded in the steady rain
on my hut

once,
seeing my smile
that did its silent work,
the master stopped
his word-flow

whether I stay
or don't,
whether I write
my article or let it pass,
I am in this Hut of the Small Mind

wanting to stay,
I could not,
and leaving,
I wanted
to write ten thousand poems

my interview-less
interview is over,
and bag in hand,
I descend
the muddy road

as if clutching
the master's
thirty-one,
I leave
Do Nothing Farm

no farewell
except
this calligraphy'd sheet,
I watch the master
trudge off in mountain rain

the balloon
he drew
with a brush
carries
all the nothingness away!

as if expelled
from further room
at the inn,
I leave
my Hut of the Small Mind

I see another
arrival
for his own three-day
as if a brief fondled *mu*
can be tucked away

in muddy trousers
and muddy shoes
I go down
the mud-filled road
from the Hut of the Small Mind

throat bearded,
I back into
the world
from Do Nothing
Farm

I drag down
the *sabi* emptiness
of my mountain hut;
in Kyoto
there's rain

changing
into another gyration
of self,
I return
to the everyday whirl

I shave away
my do-nothing life,
all the dampness
unfolded and left out to dry,
and still: that solidity on my shoes

away from
Do Nothing Farm,
and this rain-stilled
Kyoto night
is tender, is sad

the American
that took
my place,
is he watching
Rebecca's sad eyes?

it rains
on and on,
and the mountain damp
extends
even to my Kyoto bath

in a taxi
along this Kyoto street,
two hairstyles
of sumo wrestlers
from the back window . . .

www.ingramcontent.com/pod-product-compliance
Lightning Source LLC
Chambersburg PA
CBHW020951030426
42339CB00004B/52

* 9 780986 432811 *